- Snow Goose (p. 10)
- Canada Goose (p. 11) 
- Tundra Swan (p. 12)
- Wood Duck (p. 13) 
- Mallard (p. 14) 
- Bufflehead (p. 15) 
- Common Merganser (p. 16) 
- Wild Turkey (p. 17) 
- Ruffed Grouse (p. 18) 
- Red-necked Grebe (p. 19) 
- Rock Pigeon (p. 20) 
- Mourning Dove (p. 21) 
- Common Nighthawk (p. 22) 
- Ruby-throated Hummingbird (p. 23) 
- Sora (p. 24) 
- Sandhill Crane (p. 25)

2 Reference Key

Killdeer (p. 26)

Wilson's Snipe (p. 27)

Spotted Sandpiper (p. 28)

Common Murre (p. 29)

Atlantic Puffin (p. 30)

Bonaparte's Gull (p. 31)

Ring-billed Gull (p. 32)

Common Tern (p. 33)

Common Loon (p. 34)

Double-crested Cormorant (p. 35)

American White Pelican (p. 36)

Great Blue Heron (p. 37)

Reference Key 3

- Turkey Vulture (p. 38)
- Osprey (p. 39)
- Northern Harrier (p. 40)
- Sharp-shinned Hawk (p. 41)
- Bald Eagle (p. 42)
- Red-tailed Hawk (p. 43)
- Great Horned Owl (p. 44)
- Snowy Owl (p. 45)
- Barred Owl (p. 46)
- Merlin (p. 47)
- Yellow-bellied Sapsucker (p. 48)
- Downy Woodpecker (p. 49)

4 Reference Key

- Northern Flicker (p. 50)
- Pileated Woodpecker (p. 51) 
- Belted Kingfisher (p. 52) 
- Olive-sided Flycatcher (p. 53) 
- Eastern Kingbird (p. 54) 
- Red-eyed Vireo (p. 55) 
- Northern Shrike (p. 56) 
- Canada Jay (p. 57) 
- Blue Jay (p. 58) 
- American Crow (p. 59) 
- Common Raven (p. 60) 
- Black-capped Chickadee (p. 61) 
- Horned Lark (p. 62) 
- Purple Martin (p. 63) 
- Barn Swallow (p. 64)
- Ruby-crowned Kinglet (p. 65)

Reference Key 5

Cedar Waxwing (p. 66)	Red-breasted Nuthatch (p. 67)	 White-breasted Nuthatch (p. 68)	Brown Creeper (p. 69)
 House Wren (p. 70)	 Gray Catbird (p. 71)	 European Starling (p. 72)	 Eastern Bluebird (p. 73)
 American Robin (p. 74)	 House Sparrow (p. 75)	 Evening Grosbeak (p. 76)	 Purple Finch (p. 77)
 Common Redpoll (p. 78)	 Pine Siskin (p. 79)	 American Goldfinch (p. 80)	 Dark-eyed Junco (p. 81)

6 Reference Key

Chipping Sparrow (p. 82)

White-throated Sparrow (p. 83)

Song Sparrow (p. 84)

Eastern Meadowlark (p. 85)

Baltimore Oriole (p. 86)

Red-winged Blackbird (p. 87)

Brown-headed Cowbird (p. 88)

Common Grackle (p. 89)

Common Yellowthroat (p. 90)

American Redstart (p. 91)

Yellow Warbler (p. 92)

Scarlet Tanager (p. 93)

Northern Cardinal (p. 94)

Indigo Bunting (p. 95)

Introduction

Birds are a diverse and fascinating class of vertebrates. They have captured the human imagination for centuries with their remarkable adaptations, intriguing behaviours and vibrant plumage. As the only living descendants of the dinosaurs, birds are found on every continent, from the icy lands of Antarctica and the scorching deserts of Africa to the dense rainforests of the Americas. With an estimated 10,000 species, birds exhibit an astonishing array of sizes and shapes, and they fill a diverse range of ecological roles.

With its vast and varied landscapes, northeastern North America is home to a remarkable number of birds. From rugged coastlines and critical wetlands to expansive forests and Arctic tundra, this region provides habitat for more than 400 bird species. It serves as a home range, vital breeding ground, winter refuge and migratory corridor.

Species such as the common loon, with its eerie, haunting call, and the Atlantic puffin, with its adorable clownish face, find their home in this region. Expansive wetlands attract waterfowl, such as Canada geese and wood ducks, and the cheerful calls of black-capped chickadees echo throughout the forests.

Introduction

This book is not meant to be a comprehensive guide to all the birds in northeastern North America. Instead, this handy pocket guide showcases some of the more common or iconic birds that call this region home. It offers tips on how to identify them as well as where to look for them. Finding some species may require a jaunt to a national park or conservation area, but for others you need look no farther than your own backyard or local green space. Birds are all around us, and this guide will help you learn a little more about the species that we share our landscape with.

10 Snow Goose · *Anser caerulescens*

Noisy snow geese can be quite entertaining, creating a moving patchwork in the sky. With black wing tips and white plumage, groups of these birds appear like a dark cluster one moment then seemingly disappear the next when they synchronize their changes in flight direction. • These geese breed in the northern tundra. Their smiling, serrated bills are made for grazing on short arctic plants and gripping the slippery roots of marsh vegetation.
• Snow geese fly in wavy, disorganized lines, versus the V-formation of Canada Geese. Occasionally they migrate together in mixed flocks.

ID: 1. white overall **2.** dark "grin" on pink bill
Size: *Length:* 28–33 in (71–84 cm); *Wingspan:* 4 ½–5 ft (1.4–1.5 m)
Where found: croplands, fields, open areas, lakes, ponds and coastal marshes

Canada Goose · *Branta canadensis* 11

Canada geese mate for life and are devoted parents. Unlike most birds, the family stays together for nearly a year, which helps to increase the survival rate of the young. • Wild geese can be aggressive, especially when defending young or competing for food. Hissing sounds and low, outstretched necks are signs that you should give these birds some space. • These geese graze on aquatic grasses and sprouts, and you may spot them tipping up to grab aquatic roots and tubers.

ID: 1. white "chin strap" **2.** long, black neck **3.** short, black tail
Size: *Length:* 22–48 in (56–122 cm); *Wingspan:* up to 6 ft (1.8 m)
Where found: lakeshores, riverbanks, ponds, farmlands and city parks

12 Tundra Swan · *Cygnus columbianus*

Tundra swans migrate through Western Canada in spring and fall, gathering at staging areas to rest and refuel on aquatic vegetation. • Trumpeter Swans closely resemble tundras, and it can be difficult to tell them apart. Look for the yellow lores and the straighter neck of the tundra swan compared to the black lores and S-curved neck of the trumpeter.

ID: 1. yellow lores **2.** large, black bill **3.** neck is held straight up **4.** white plumage
Size: *Length:* 4–5 ft (1.2–1.5 m); *Wingspan:* 5 ft (1.5 m)
Where found: shallow areas of lakes and wetlands, agricultural fields and flooded pastures

Wood Duck · *Aix sponsa* 13

Wood ducks nest in tree cavities. Thousands of nest boxes placed across their breeding range have greatly increased populations.
- Shortly after hatching, ducklings jump out of their nest cavity, often falling more than 20 ft (6 m) to bounce harmlessly like ping pong balls on landing.
- Females often return to the same nest site year after year, especially after successfully raising a brood.

ID: *Male:* **1.** long, slicked back, greenish crest edged with white **2.** red eyes **3.** white throat, neck ring and facial 'spur' **4.** mostly reddish bill **5.** rusty breast with small white spots *Female:* **6.** white teardrop-shaped eye patch
Size: *Length:* 15–21 in (38–53 cm); *Wingspan:* 30–33 in (76–84 cm)
Where found: swamps, ponds, marshes, rivers and lake shores with wooded edges

14 Mallard · *Anas platyrhynchos*

The male mallard, with his shiny green head and chestnut brown breast, is the classic wild duck. Mallards can be seen year-round, often in flocks and always near open water. • Most people think the mallard's quack is a typical duck call, but few ducks actually make quacking sounds. Surprisingly, the croak of a male wood frog sounds similar to a mallard's call, so don't be fooled in early spring.

breeding

ID: *Male:* **1.** glossy, green head **2.** yellow bill **3.** chestnut brown breast
Female: **4.** orange bill is spattered with black **5.** mottled brown overall
Size: *Length:* 20–28 in (51–71 cm); *Wingspan:* 31–35 in (78–89 cm)
Where found: lakes, wetlands, rivers, city parks, stormwater ponds, agricultural areas and sewage lagoons

Bufflehead · *Bucephala albeola*

The tiny bufflehead might be the first diving duck you learn to identify. The striking white patch on the rear of the male's head stands out, even at a distance. • Buffleheads nest in tree cavities, using abandoned woodpecker nests or natural holes. They are small enough to squeeze into holes only 3 in (8 cm) wide! After hatching, the ducklings remain in the nest chamber for up to three days before jumping out and tumbling to the ground.

ID: *Female:* **1.** white, oval ear patch
Male: **2.** white wedge on back of head
3. iridescent, dark green or purple head usually appears black
Size: *Length:* 13–15 in (33–38 cm); *Wingspan:* 21 in (53 cm)
Where found: open water of lakes, large ponds and rivers; coastal bays and estuaries

16 Common Merganser · *Mergus merganser*

Merganser drakes ride low in the water. They are noticeably larger than most other duck species and are also one of our heaviest ducks, tipping the scales at 3½ lbs (1.6 kg). • Mergansers have bills that are sharply serrated like carving knives, designed to catch and hold their fishy prey. • Outside the breeding season mergansers are highly social, forming large flocks.

ID: *Male:* **1.** glossy, green head without crest **2.** blood red bill
Female: **3.** rusty neck and crested head **4.** orange bill **5.** clean white "chin" and breast
Size: *Length:* 22–27 in (56–69 cm); *Wingspan:* 34 in (86 cm)
Where found: large forest-lined rivers, deep lakes and reservoirs

Wild Turkey · *Meleagris gallopavo*

The once common wild turkey suffered habitat loss and overhunting in the early 20th century. Today restoration efforts have re-established the species in many areas, including urban greenbelts. • This charismatic bird is the only widely domesticated native North American animal. The wild ancestors of most other domestic animals come from Europe. • Although turkeys prefer to feed on the ground and travel by foot, they can fly short distances, and they normally roost high in trees during the night.

ID: 1. unfeathered head 2. dark, glossy, iridescent body plumage
Male: 3. long, central beard on breast
4. blueish head and red wattles
Size: *Male Length:* 4–4 ¼ ft (1.2–1.3 m);
Wingspan: 5 ¼ ft (1.6 m);
Female Length: 35–41 in (89–104 cm);
Wingspan: 4 ¼ in (1.3 m)
Where found: open, mixed word valleys, a plans with shrubby areas and agricultural lands

18 Ruffed Grouse · *Bonasa umbellus*

If you hear a loud booming echoing through the forest in early spring, you are likely listening to a male ruffed grouse "drumming" to announce his territory. Every spring, and occasionally in fall, the male grouse struts along a fallen log with his tail fanned and his neck feathers ruffed, beating the air with accelerating wing strokes. • In winter, feather-like scales grow out along the sides of this grouse's feet, creating temporary "snowshoes." Only grouse and ptarmigan have this specialized feature.

ID: *Male, grey morph:* **1.** small, pointed head crest **2.** mottled, grey-brown overall **3.** grey- or reddish-barred tail has broad, dark, subterminal band and white tip
Size: *Length:* 15–19 in (38–48 cm); *Wingspan:* 22 in (56 cm)
Where found: deciduous and mixed forests and riparian woodlands; favours young stands with birch and poplar

Red-necked Grebe · *Podiceps grisegena*

breeding

Nesting red-necked grebes are usually noticed because of their frequent, raucous, braying calls, which end in a horse-like whinny. • These grebes are highly territorial and aggressive, often threatening or making underwater attack dives against other waterbirds that enter their territory. • Grebes have individually webbed, or "lobed," feet. The three forward-facing toes have special flanges that are not connected to the other toes.

ID: 1. black crown **2.** white "cheek" **3.** rusty neck **4.** straight, heavy bill is dark above and yellow underneath
Size: *Length:* 17–22 (43–56 cm); *Wingspan:* 30–33 in (76–84 cm)
Where found: open, deep lakes

20 Rock Pigeon · *Columba livia*

Birds lack mammary glands, but the familiar rock pigeon has an unusual feature. This bird feeds its young "pigeon milk," a nutritious liquid produced in the crop. A chick inserts its bill down the adult's throat to reach the thick, protein-rich fluid. • Rock pigeons are likely the descendants of a Eurasian bird that was first domesticated around 4500 BC. They have been used as message couriers by the likes of Caesar and Napoleon, as scientific subjects and even as pets.

ID: 1. colour is highly variable (iridescent blue grey, red, white or tan) **2.** dark-tipped tail **3.** usually has white rump
Size: *Length:* 12–13 in (30–33 cm); *Wingspan:* 28 in (71 cm)
Where found: urban areas, railway yards and agricultural areas; high cliffs often provide more natural habitat

Mourning Dove · *Zenaida macroura*

When the mourning dove's soft cooing filters through woodlands and suburban parks, it is often confused with the sound of a hooting owl. • These popular game animals are some of the most abundant native birds in North America. Their numbers and range have increased since human development created more open habitats and food sources, such as waste grain and bird feeders.

ID: 1. dark, shiny patch below ear **2.** pale rosy underparts **3.** long, white-trimmed, tapering tail **4.** black spots on upperwing
Size: *Length:* 11–13 in (28–33 cm); *Wingspan:* 18 in (46 cm)
Where found: open and riparian woodlands, forest edges, agricultural and suburban areas, open parks

22 Common Nighthawk · *Chordeiles minor*

The common nighthawk makes an unforgettable booming sound as it flies high overhead. The courting male dives, then swerves skyward, making a hollow vroom sound with its wings. • This bird has adapted to catch insects in midair. Its gaping beak is surrounded by feather shafts that funnel insects into its mouth. A nighthawk can eat over 2600 insects in one day.

ID: 1. cryptic, mottled plumage **2.** tiny bill **3.** barred underparts *Male:* **4.** white throat on male
Size: *Length:* 9–10 (23–25 cm); *Wingspan:* 24 (61 cm)
Where found: *Breeding:* large forest openings, burns, bogs, rocky outcroppings and gravel rooftops. *In migration:* often near water

Ruby-throated Hummingbird · *Archilochus colubris*

Ruby-throated hummingbirds feed on sweet, energy-rich flower nectar and pollinate the flowers in the process. A sugarwater feeder or native, nectar-producing flowers such as honeysuckle can attract hummingbirds to your backyard. • Each year, these hummingbirds migrate across the Gulf of Mexico, a nonstop 500 mile (800 km) journey. Weighing about as much as a nickel, they can briefly reach speeds of up to 62 miles (100 km) per hour!

ID: 1. needle-like bill **2.** pale underparts
Male: **3.** dark tail **4.** black "chin" with ruby red throat
Size: *Length:* 3–4 in; (8–10 cm); *Wingspan:* 4 ¾ in (12 cm)
Where found: open, mixed woodlands, orchards, tree-lined meadows, wetlands, flower gardens and backyards with trees and feeders

24 Sora · *Porzana carolina*

Soras have small bodies and large, chickenlike feet. Even without webbed feet, these unique creatures swim quite well over short distances. • Two rising *or-Ah or-Ah* whistles followed by a strange, descending whinny indicate that soras are nearby. • Although the sora is the most common and widespread rail species in North America, it is seldom seen. This secretive bird prefers to remain hidden in dense marshland, but it will occasionally venture into the shallows to search for aquatic insects and molluscs.

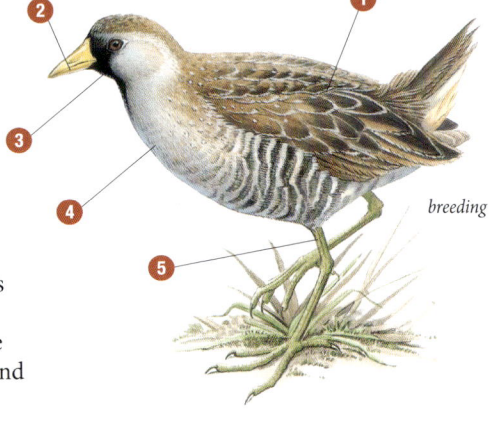

breeding

ID: *Breeding:* **1.** brown, white-speckled back and upper wings **2.** short, yellow bill **3.** black face, throat and foreneck **4.** grey neck and breast **5.** long, greenish legs
Size: *Length:* 8–10 in (20–25 cm); *Wingspan:* 13 ¾ in (35 cm)
Where found: wetlands with abundant emergent cattails, bulrushes, sedges and grasses

Sandhill Crane · *Antigone canadensis*

The sandhill crane's deep, rattling call can be heard long before this bird passes overhead. Its coiled trachea alters the pitch of its voice, making it sound louder and carry farther. • At first glance, large, V-shaped flocks of sandhill cranes can look like flocks of Canada geese, but the cranes often soar and circle in the air, and they do not honk like geese. • Cranes mate for life and reinforce pair bonds each spring with an elaborate courtship dance.

ID: 1. long neck **2.** naked, red crown **3.** long, straight bill **4.** grey overall
Size: *Length:* 3 ¼–4 ¼ ft (1–1.3 m); *Wingspan:* 6–7 ft (1.8–2.1 m)
Where found: open ground, fields, lakeshores, sandy beaches, mudflats, gravel streambeds, wet meadows

26 Killdeer · *Charadrius vociferus*

The killdeer is well known for its "broken wing" distraction display. When an intruder wanders too close to its nest, the killdeer cries piteously while dragging a wing and stumbling about as if injured. Most predators take the bait and follow, and once the killdeer has lured the predator far away from its nest, it "recovers" from the "injury" and flies off with a loud call.

ID: 1. brown back and head 2. white "eyebrow" 3. 2 black breast bands 4. white underparts 5. long, dark yellow legs
Size: *Length:* 9–11 in (23–28 cm); *Wingspan:* 19–21 (48–53 cm)
Where found: open ground, fields, lakeshores, sandy beaches, mudflats, gravel streambeds, wet meadows and grasslands

Wilson's Snipe · *Gallinago delicata*

A courting Wilson's Snipe makes an eerie, winnowing sound, like a rapidly hooting owl. The male's specialized outer tail feathers vibrate rapidly in the air as he dives headfirst, high above wetlands. During the spring, snipes can be heard displaying day and night. • These birds use a zigzagging flight to confuse predators. Because of this habit, hunters who were skilled enough to shoot snipes became known as "snipers," a term later adopted by the military.

ID: 1. dark eye stripe **2.** heavily striped head **3.** long, sturdy, bicoloured bill
Size: *Length:* 10 ½–11 ½ in (27–29 cm); *Wingspan:* 17 ¼–20 in (44–51 cm)
Where found: cattail and bulrush marshes, sedge meadows, poorly drained floodplains, bogs and fens, swamps and edges of farm fields

28 Spotted Sandpiper · *Actitis macularius*

During breeding season, you can expect to see the spotted sandpiper almost anywhere in Canada, from sea level to the barren alpine tundra. Like a handful of other shorebirds, the female spotted sandpiper is the more aggressive partner in courtship. The male takes of raising the chicks. Each summer, the female can lay up to four clutches. • Sandpipers have four toes: three point forward and one points backward. Plovers, such as killdeer, have only three toes.

breeding

ID: *Breeding:* **1.** white "eyebrow" **2.** black-tipped, yellow orange bill **3.** white underparts heavily spotted with black **4.** yellow orange legs
Size: *Length:* 7–8 in (18–20 cm); *Wingspan:* 14–15 in (36–38 cm
Where found: shorelines, gravel beaches, ponds, marshes, alluvial wetlands, rivers, streams, swamps and sewage lagoons

Common Murre · *Uria aalge*

Common murres spend much of their lives at sea and only come ashore to breed. They nest in huge, tightly packed colonies on isolated coastal cliffs, stacks and offshore islands. Some sites support tens of thousands of birds. • Murres can remain beneath the surface for more than a minute and regularly dive to depths of 100 ft (30 m). These skilled swimmers use their small wings, webbed feet and sleek, waterproof plumage to pursue fish underwater.

breeding

nonbreeding

ID: *Breeding:* **1.** slender, black bill **2.** deep, sooty brown upperparts **3.** white underparts
Size: *Length:* 16 ¼–17 in (41–43 cm); *Wingspan:* 26 in (66 cm)
Where found: *Breeding:* on offshore islands, islets and rocks. *Foraging:* on open ocean from just beyond the surf zone to far offshore

Atlantic Puffin · *Fratercula arctica*

The Atlantic puffin can line up more than a dozen small fish crosswise in its bill, possibly using its round tongue and serrated upper mandible to keep the hoard in place. Even so, capturing more fish without losing all previous catches must take great skill! • Parents abandon their nest burrow when the nestling is about 40 days old. After a week of fasting, the nestling ventures out to the ocean, fully capable of feeding itself.

breeding

ID: *Breeding:* **1.** white face **2.** orange bill with triangular, grey patch, bordered by yellow **3.** orange legs
Size: *Length:* 13 in (33 cm); *Wingspan:* 21 (53 cm)
Where found: *Breeding:* inaccessible coastal cliffs and offshore islands with turf. *In migration and winter:* open ocean, occasionally inshore

Bonaparte's Gull · *Chroicocephalus philadelphia*

The Bonaparte's gull avoids landfills, preferring to dine on insects caught in midair or plucked from the water's surface. • This small gull is unlike any other gull or tern in that it nests in the upper branches of coniferous trees. Nesting solitarily or in very loose colonies, it often chooses a site that is close to water. • The phrase "black-bill Bonaparte's" is a useful memory aid for identification.

breeding

nonbreeding

ID: 1. black head **2.** black bill **3.** white eye ring **4.** orangish-red legs
Size: *Length:* 12–14 in (30–36 cm); *Wingspan:* 33 in (84 cm)
Habitat: *Breeding:* coniferous forests, bordering lakes. *In migration and winter:* large lakes, rivers and marine nearshore upwellings

Ring-billed Gull · *Larus delawarensis*

The ring-billed gull is the most widespread and abundant inland-nesting gull in North America. Highly tolerant of humans, it has become a routine sight at many shopping mall parking lots, sports fields, beaches and city parks. • In rural settings, these gulls follow agricultural machinery to feast on crop pests. • Ring-bills are a three-year gull, meaning that it takes them three full seasons to acquire the characteristic grey-and-white plumage of adults.

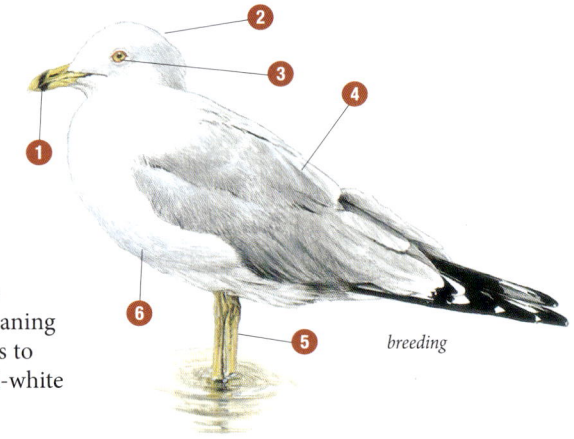

breeding

nonbreeding

ID: 1. black ring on yellow bill **2.** white head **3.** yellow eyes **4.** pale grey mantle **5.** yellow legs **6.** white underparts
Size: Length: 46–51 cm; *Wingspan:* 1.2 m
Where found: lakes, rivers, landfills, golf courses, fields and parks

Common Tern · *Sterna hirundo*

Common terns are sleek, agile birds that patrol shorelines and shallows of lakes and rivers looking for small fish. • These terns spend the winter in British Columbia, then migrate east of the Rocky Mountains to breed. They settle in large, noisy nesting colonies. • To win a mate, the male struts around with an offering of fish in his mouth. If a female accepts his gift, the two make a breeding pair. The pair defends their nest by diving repeatedly and aggressively at intruders to drive them away.

breeding

ID: 1. black cap **2.** black tip on red bill **3.** red legs **4.** pale grey mantle
Size: *Length:* 13–16 ¼ in (33–41 cm); *Wingspan:* 30 in (76 cm)
Where found: large lakes, open wetlands, slow-moving rivers, islands and beaches

34 Common Loon · *Gavia immer*

Common loons are well suited to their aquatic lifestyle. Most birds have hollow bones, but loons have solid bones that reduce their buoyancy and make diving easier. They can dive up to 165 ft (50 m) deep in pursuit of fish. • Loons have several different calls. Frightened loons give a laughing distress call, separated pairs seem to wail *where aaare you?* and groups give soft, cohesive hoots as they fly.

breeding

ID: 1. green-black head **2.** black-and-white "checkerboard" upperparts **3.** red eyes **4.** white "necklace" **5.** stout, thick, black bill
Size: *Length:* 28–35 in (71–89 cm); *Wingspan:* 4–5 ft (1.2–1.5 m)
Where found: large lakes, often with islands that provide undisturbed shorelines for nesting

Double-crested Cormorant · *Nannopterum auritum*

breeding

The double-crested cormorant is named for its nuptial crests, small eyebrow plumes the birds sport during the breeding season.

These plumes are black on birds in the east and white on birds in the west. • This bird has sealed nostrils for diving and therefore must occasionally open its bill to breathe while in flight. • Most water birds have waterproof feathers, but the cormorant's unique feathers allow water in. This decreases buoyancy and makes diving easier. After a swim, the cormorant will perch in a tree or stand on the ground with its wings spread out so its feathers can dry.

ID: 1. fine, plumes trail from "eyebrows" **2.** thin bill, hooked at tip **3.** all-black body **4.** yellowish-orange throat pouch **5.** long, crooked neck
Size: *Length:* 26–32 in (66–82 cm); *Wingspan:* 4 1/4 ft (1.3 m)
Where found: large lakes and large, meandering rivers

American White Pelican · *Pelecanus erythrorhynchos*

This majestic wetland bird is one of only a few bird species that feeds cooperatively. A group of pelicans will herd fish into a school, then dip their bucket-like bills into the water to capture their prey. In a single scoop, a pelican can trap over 3 gal (12 L) of water and fish in its bill, which is about two to three times as much as its stomach can hold. • The feathers on a pelican's wing tips are black and have a pigment called melanin that doesn't wear in the wind.

nonbreeding

ID: 1. naked orange skin patch around eye **2.** long, orange bill and throat pouch **3.** white plumage is tinged brown
Size: *Length:* 4 ½–6 ft (1.4–1.8 m); *Wingspan:* 9 ft (2.7 m)
Where found: lakes, river mouths and marshes, occasionally in city ponds

Great Blue Heron · *Ardea herodias* 37

The long-legged great blue heron has a stealthy, often motionless hunting strategy. It waits for a fish or frog to approach, spears the prey with its bill, then flips its catch into the air and swallows it whole. • Herons usually hunt near water, but they also stalk fields and meadows in search of rodents. • Great blue herons settle in communal treetop nests called rookeries. Nesting herons are sensitive to human disturbance, so observe this bird's behaviour from a distance.

ID: 1. blue-grey overall **2.** straight, yellow bill **3.** long, curving neck with black markings on throat **4.** chestnut brown thighs **5.** long, dark legs
Size: *Length:* 4 ¼–4 ½ ft (1.3–1.4 m); *Wingspan:* 6 ft (1.8 m)
Where found: forages along edges of rivers, lakes, marshes, fields and wet meadows

38 Turkey Vulture · *Cathartes aura*

Turkey vultures are intelligent, social birds. Groups live and sleep together in large trees, or roosts. Some roost sites are more than a century old and have been used by the same family of vultures for several generations.

- Vultures have an affinity for carrion because their bills and feet are much less powerful than those of eagles, hawks or falcons, which kill live prey. The turkey vulture's red, featherless head allows the bird to stay relatively clean while feeding on messy carcasses.

ID: 1. bare, red head **2.** pale, hooked bill **3.** all-black plumage
Size: *Length:* 25–31 ½ in (64–80 cm); *Wingspan:* 5 ½–6 ft (1.7–1.8 m)
Where found: hunts over open country, transmission corridors and shorelines; nests in forests and on rocky bluffs.

Osprey · *Pandion haliaetus*

The osprey is a unique member of the raptor family. With an almost exclusively fish diet, this "fish hawk" has mastered one of the most impressive dives of the avian world. From more than 100 ft (30 m) high, it dives headfirst and then rights itself and thrusts its feet forward moments before hitting the water. It emerges with prey caught in its specialized talons—two toes face forward and two face backward with spines for clamping slippery fish. • After the banning of DDT in the early 1970s, Osprey numbers have greatly increased—a true environmental success story.

ID: 1. dark eye line **2.** long wings extend past tail **3.** white underparts with variable spotting on breast
Size: *Length:* 22–25 in (56–64 cm); *Wingspan:* 4 ½–6 ft (1.4–1.8 m)
Where found: lakes, large wetlands and slow moving rivers

40 Northern Harrier · *Circus hudsonius*

With its prominent white rump and wings held in a V-shape, the northern harrier may be the easiest raptor to identify in flight. Unlike other midsized birds, it often glides low to the ground, relying on sudden surprise attacks to capture prey. • With its prominent facial discs to better detect and focus sounds, a perched harrier looks astonishingly like an owl.

ID: 1. prominent facial disc.
Male: **2.** faintly streaked white underparts **3.** grey upperparts.
Female: **4.** brown-streaked buffy underparts **5.** brown upperparts
Size: *Length:* 16 ¼ –24 in (41–61 cm); *Wingspan:* 3 ½–4 ft (1.1–1.2 m)
Where found: open country, including fields, wet meadows, cattail marshes, bogs and croplands

Sharp-shinned Hawk · *Accipiter striatus*

Sharpies are the smallest members of the *Accipiter* genus, or woodland hawks, and prey almost exclusively on small birds. Their short, rounded wings, long, rudderlike tails and flap-and-glide flight pattern allow them to manoeuvre through the forest at high speed. • After a successful hunt, the small sharp-shinned hawk often perches on a favourite "plucking post" with its meal in its razor-sharp talons. • As with most hawks, females are noticeably larger than males.

ID: 1. blue-grey crown **2.** red horizontal bars on underparts **3.** long, heavily barred, square-tipped tail

Size: *Male Length:* 10–12 in (25–30 cm); *Wingspan:* 20–24 in (51–61 cm). *Female Length:* 12–14 in (30–36 cm); *Wingspan:* 24–28 in (61–71 cm)

Where found: dense to semi-open forests and large woodlots; occasionally along rivers and in urban areas; favours bogs and dense, moist, forests for nesting

42 Bald Eagle · *Haliaeetus leucocephalus*

Part of the sea eagle group, the majestic bald eagle feeds mostly on fish and is often found near water. While soaring high in the air, this eagle can spot fish swimming underwater and small rodents scurrying through the grass. It also scavenges carrion and steals food from other birds. • Bald eagles do not mature until their fourth or fifth year—only then will they develop the characteristic white head and tail plumage.

adult

ID: 1. white head **2.** yellow bill **3.** dark brown body **4.** yellow feet
Size: *Length:* 30–44 in (76–110 cm); *Wingspan:* 5 ½–8 ft (1.7–2.4 m)
Where found: large lakes and rivers

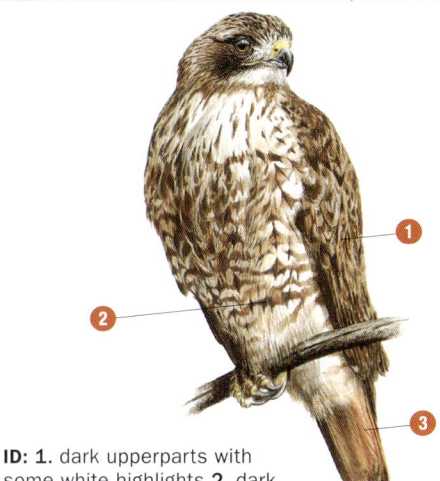

Red-tailed Hawk · *Buteo jamaicensis*

Red-tailed hawks are found virtually everywhere in western Canada, from farmland to forest, sea level to alpine. • In warm weather, these hawks use thermals and updrafts to soar. These pockets of rising air provide substantial lift, which allows migrating hawks to save energy and to fly for great distances without flapping their wings. • Red-tails eat small mammals and medium-sized birds as well as snakes, lizards and frogs.

ID: 1. dark upperparts with some white highlights **2.** dark brown band of streaks across belly **3.** red tail
Size: *Male Length:* 18–23 in (46–58 cm); *Wingspan:* 3 ½–5 ft (1.1–1.5 m). *Female Length:* 20–25 in (51–64 cm); *Wingspan:* 3 ½–5 ft (1.1–1.5 m)
Where found: open country with some trees; also roadsides, fields or woodlots

44 Great Horned Owl · *Bubo virginianus*

The great horned owl is highly adaptable and widespread, even occurring in urban areas. This powerful predator hunts at night and by day, using its sharp hearing and powerful vision to locate prey. It will eat any small creature, including house cats and skunks. • Great horned owls build large stick nests and may be spotted by their "ears" projecting above the nest. Courtship begins in early January, with females incubating their eggs by February and March.

ID: 1. rusty orange facial disc is outlined in black **2.** yellow eyes **3.** wide-set "ear" tufts **4.** fine, horizontal barring on breast
Size: *Length:* 18–25 in (46–64 cm); *Wingspan:* 3 ¼–4 ¼ ft (1–1.3 m)
Where found: fragmented forests, fields, riparian woodlands, suburban parks and wooded edges of landfills

Snowy Owl · *Bubo scandiacus*

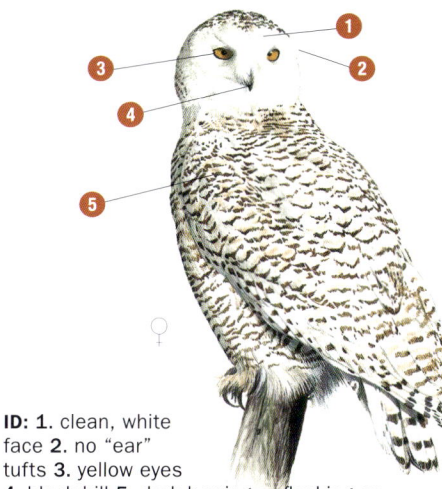

Feathered to the toes, the snowy owl can remain active even in frigid winter temperatures. Its plumage traps heat like a greenhouse. This bird also creates insulating air pockets between its body and the cold air by ruffling its feathers. • Snowy owls are regular winter visitors across Canada, but their numbers can fluctuate dramatically. When lemming and vole populations crash in the Arctic, large numbers of snowy owls venture south to search for food. • As these owls age, their plumage becomes lighter. Males are also lighter, so pure white owls are almost certainly older males.

ID: 1. clean, white face **2.** no "ear" tufts **3.** yellow eyes **4.** black bill **5.** dark barring or flecking on breast and upperparts
Size: *Length:* 20–28 in (51–71 cm); *Wingspan:* 4–5 ft (1.2–1.5 m)
Where found: open country, including croplands, meadows and lakeshores; often perches on fence posts, buildings and utility poles

Barred Owl · *Strix varia*

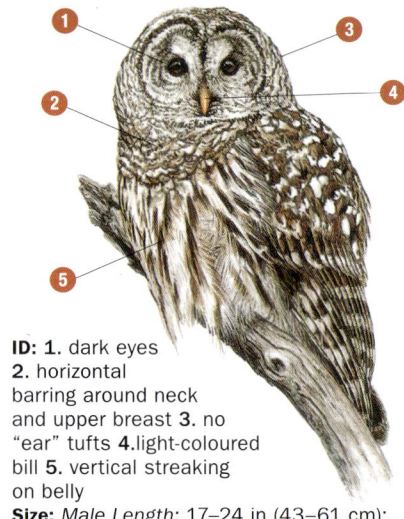

The remarkably adaptable barred owl is found in many woodland habitats, especially those near water. Increasingly, these owls are turning up in suburban forests. • Barred owls reinforce pair bonds each spring. Their typical call is a series of hoots that sound like *Who cooks for you? Who cooks for you?* They tend to be more vocal at dawn and dusk, when the moon is full and the sky is clear.

ID: 1. dark eyes **2**. horizontal barring around neck and upper breast **3**. no "ear" tufts **4**. light-coloured bill **5**. vertical streaking on belly

Size: *Male Length:* 17–24 in (43–61 cm); *Wingspan:* 3 ¼–4 ¼ ft (1.0–1.3 m) *Female Length:* 22–24 in (56–61 cm); *Wingspan:* 3 ½–4 ¼ ft (1.1–1.3 m)

Where found: mature coniferous and mixedwood forests, especially in dense stands near swamps, streams and lakes

Merlin · *Falco columbarius*

The merlin snatches small songbirds and shorebirds in mid-air at high speed, in classic falcon fashion. • Merlins seldom perch on power lines and usually hunt from a snag or other conspicuous perch. Rural cemeteries and parks with mature spruce trees are good places to look for these birds. • The former name "pigeon hawk" refers to the bird's appearance in flight, not its preferred prey. Although the merlin will take rock pigeons, it mostly hunts smaller prey like small songbirds and shorebirds.

ID: 1. vertical facial stripe **2.** dark eye line **3.** heavy brown streaking on pale underparts
Female: **4.** dark brown upperparts
Male: **5.** blue-grey upperparts
Size: *Length:* 10–12 in (25–30 cm); *Wingspan:* 23–26 in (58–66 cm)
Where found: treed areas next to open hunting grounds; also suburban areas and lakeshores

48 Yellow-bellied Sapsucker · *Sphyrapicus varius*

Yellow-bellied sapsuckers make their presence known in May, when their irregular tapping echoes throughout our woodlands. Listen for pairs rapping in rhythmic duets. • Sapsuckers drill "wells" in tree trunks, which fill with sweet, sticky sap and attract insects. The sapsuckers eat both the trapped bugs and the pooled sap and must defend the wells from other wildlife, including hummingbirds and small rodents. A pair of sapsuckers might drill many sites within their territory.

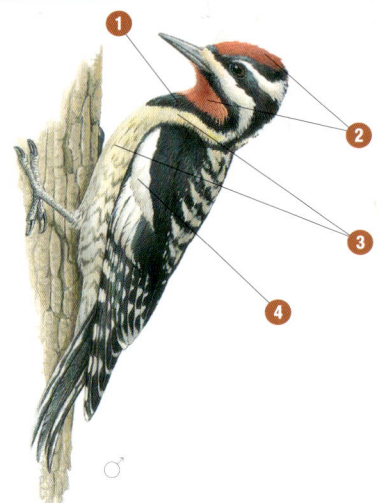

ID: *Male:* **1.** black "bib" **2.** red forecrown and "chin" **3.** yellow wash on lower breast and belly **4.** large, white wing patch
Size: *Length:* 7–8 in (18–20 cm); *Wingspan:* 16 in (40 cm)
Where found: deciduous and mixed forests, especially dry, second-growth woodlands

Downy Woodpecker · *Dryobates pubescens* 49

The downy woodpecker is the smallest North American woodpecker and the most likely to be found in neighbourhood ravines or visiting feeders. • It closely resembles the hairy woodpecker but is much smaller, with a comparatively tiny bill and black spots on the white outer tail feathers. • Woodpeckers have evolved special features to help cushion the shock of repeated hammering, including a strong bill and neck muscles, a flexible, reinforced skull and a brain that is tightly packed in its protective cranium.

ID: 1. short, stubby bill **2.** black wings have white bars **3.** white back **4.** *Male:* small, red patch on back of head
Size: *Length:* 6–7 in (15–18 cm); *Wingspan:* 12 in (30 cm)
Where found: any wooded environment, especially deciduous and mixed forests and areas with tall, deciduous shrubs

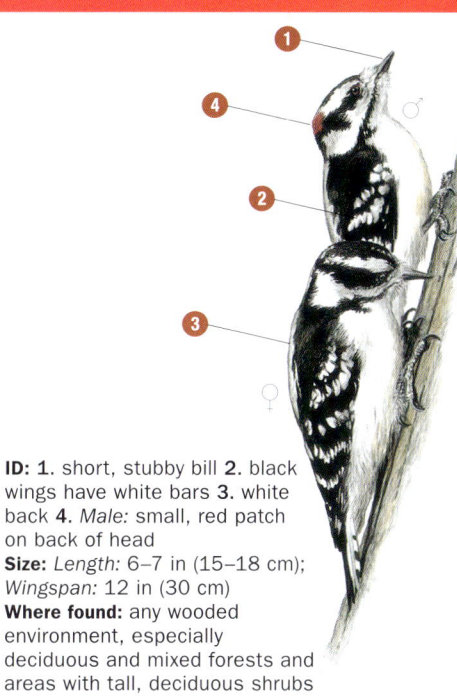

Northern Flicker · *Colaptes auratus*

Look for this woodpecker hopping on the ground in search of ants and other insects. • In flight, the northern flicker can be identified by its bold white rump patch and its undulating flight pattern. • Flickers clean themselves by squashing ants and preening themselves with the remains. Ants contain formic acid, which kills parasites on the birds' skin and feathers. • There are two flicker subspecies in western Canada: the "red-shafted" has salmon-coloured underwings and the "yellow-shafted" has yellow underwings.

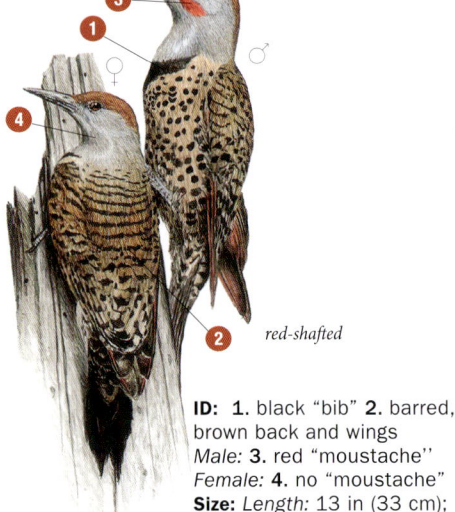

red-shafted

ID: **1.** black "bib" **2.** barred, brown back and wings *Male:* **3.** red "moustache" *Female:* **4.** no "moustache" **Size:** *Length:* 13 in (33 cm); *Wingspan:* 20 in (51 cm)
Where found: open deciduous, mixed and coniferous woodlands and forest edges, fields, meadows, beaver ponds and other wetlands

Pileated Woodpecker · *Dryocopus pileatus* 51

The pileated woodpecker, with its flaming red crest, chisel-like bill and commanding size, requires 100 acres (40 hectares) of mature forest as a home territory. Pairs may spend up to six weeks excavating a large nest cavity in a dead or decaying tree. • Woodpeckers have feathered nostrils, which filter out the sawdust produced when hammering trees. Many woodpeckers also have zygodactyl feet—two toes face forward and two point backward. This structure allows them to move vertically up and down tree trunks.

ID: 1. red crest **2.** stout, dark bill **3.** white stripe extends from bill to shoulder
Male: **4.** red "moustache"
Female: **5.** grey-black forecrown
Size: *Length:* 16 ¼–20 in (41–51 cm); *Wingspan:* 27–30 in (69–76 cm)
Where found: mature forests, riparian woodlands or woodlots in suburban and agricultural areas

52 Belted Kingfisher · *Megaceryle alcyon*

Perched on a bare branch over a productive pool, the belted kingfisher utters a scratchy, rattling call and then plunges headfirst into the water and snags a fish or frog. Back on land, the kingfisher flips its prey into the air and swallows it headfirst. • Kingfisher pairs nest on sandy banks, taking turns digging a tunnel with their sturdy bills and claws. Nest burrows may measure up to 6 ½ ft (2 m) long and are often found near water.

ID: 1. shaggy crest 2. white "collar" 3. blue upperparts 4. long, straight bill. *Male:* 5. blue-grey breast band. *Female:* 6. rust-coloured "belt" may be incomplete
Size: *Length:* 11–14 in (28–36 cm); *Wingspan:* 20 in (51 cm)
Where found: rivers, large streams, lakes, marshes and beaver ponds, especially near exposed soil banks, gravel pits or bluffs

Olive-sided Flycatcher · *Contopus cooperi*

Olive-sided flycatchers nest high in the forest canopy. Far above the forest floor, they have easy access to an abundance of flying insects, including honeybees and adult wood-boring and bark beetles. • These birds are fierce nest defenders and will harass and chase off squirrels and other predators. • A big-headed silhouette on the tip of a mature conifer or dead branch may well belong to this feisty flycatcher.

ID: 1. olive-grey to olive-brown upperparts **2.** light throat and belly **3.** dark, olive grey "vest"
Size: *Length:* 7 ½ in (19 cm); *Wingspan:* 13 in (33 cm)
Where found: semi-open mixed and coniferous forests near water; prefers burned areas and wetlands

54 Eastern Kingbird · *Tyrannus tyrannus*

The eastern kingbird fearlessly attacks crows, hawks and even humans that pass through its territory, pursuing and pecking at intruders until the threat has passed. This behaviour gives the bird its scientific name, *Tyrannus tyrannus*. • Eastern kingbirds are common and widespread, and are often seen along country roads, sitting on a fence or utility wire. • This bird eats more than 200 kinds of insects and will hover above shrubs or trees to pick berries.

ID: 1. small head crest **2.** black bill **3.** thin, orange red crown (rarely seen) **4.** dark grey to black upperparts **5.** white-tipped tail **6.** white underparts
Size: *Length:* 8 ¾ in (22 cm); *Wingspan:* 15 in (38 cm)
Where found: open areas with willow and birch shrubs, agricultural areas and riparian regions, roadsides, burned areas and near human settlement

Red-eyed Vireo · *Vireo olivaceus* 55

The male red-eyed vireo can out-sing other birds. Males can deliver about 40 phrases per minute and sing all day, from dawn to dusk. If you hear a bird singing during mid-afternoon, it is likely this vireo. Its incessant singing has earned this bird the nickname "preacher bird." • This vireo is one of the most common birds whose nests are parasitized by the brown-headed cowbird. • The red-eyed vireo perches with a hunched stance and hops with its body turned diagonally to its direction of travel. Its unique red eyes are tricky to spot without a good pair of binoculars.

breeding

ID: 1. red eyes **2.** blue-grey crown **3.** white "eyebrow" **4.** dark eye line **5.** white to pale grey underparts
Size: *Length:* 6 in (15 cm); *Wingspan:* 10 in (25 cm)
Where found: deciduous woodlands with a shrubby understorey

Northern Shrike · *Lanius borealis*

One of the fiercest predators in the songbird world, the northern shrike relies on its sharp, hooked bill to catch and kill small birds or rodents. Its tendency to impale its prey on thorns and barbs for later consumption has earned it the name "butcher bird." Shrikes are the world's only true carnivorous songbirds.
• Northern shrikes typically perch at the tops of tall trees to survey the surrounding area for prey.

ID: 1. black "mask" does not extend above hooked bill **2.** pale lower mandible **3.** white outer tail feathers
Size: *Length:* 10 in (25 cm); *Wingspan:* 15 in (38 cm)
Where found: open country, including fields, shrubby areas, forest clearings and roadsides

Canada Jay · *Perisoreus canadensis*

The Canada jay is well known for making itself at home at picnics or campsites and stealing scraps of food off unattended plates. • These jays lay their eggs as early as late February, ensuring the nestlings will get the first foods of spring, and allowing plenty of time for the young birds to learn how to forage and store food. • These birds cache food for winter, and their specialized salivary glands coat the food with a sticky mucus that helps to preserve it and make it unappetizing to other birds or mammals that might try to steal it.

ID: 1. dark grey nape and upperparts
2. fluffy, pale grey underparts **3.** long tail
Size: *Length:* 11 ½ in (29 cm);
Wingspan: 18 in (46 cm)
Where found: dense and open coniferous and mixed forests, bogs and fens; picnic sites and campgrounds

58 Blue Jay · *Cyanocitta cristata*

The blue jay is easily recognizable by its blue plumage, conspicuous crest and sharply defined facial features. Individual birds can be recognized by their characteristic head patterns. • Jays can be loud and quite aggressive when competing for sunflower seeds or peanuts at backyard feeders, driving away smaller birds, squirrels and house cats. • Blue jays imitate other sounds and often mimics the calls of hawks. • Blue jays store food from feeders in trees and other places for later use.

ID: 1. blue crest 2. black "necklace" 3. white bars and flecking on wings 4. dark bars and white corners on blue tail
Size: *Length:* 11–12 in (28–30 cm); *Wingspan:* 16 ¼ in (41 cm)
Where found: mixed deciduous forests, agricultural areas, scrubby fields and townsites

American Crow · *Corvus brachyrhynchos*

These wary, clever birds are impressive mimics, able to whine like a dog and laugh or cry like a human. • Crows are family-oriented, and the young from the previous year help their parents to raise the next year's nestlings. • American crows are ecological generalists, able to adapt to a variety of habitats. • Their diets are also variable, consisting of carrion, other bird's eggs and nestlings, seeds, berries and human food waste.

ID: 1. glossy, purple black plumage **2.** black bill **3.** square-shaped tail **4.** black legs
Size: *Length:* 17–21 in (43–53 cm); *Wingspan:* 37 in (95 cm)
Where found: urban areas, agricultural fields and other open areas with scattered woodlands, marshes, lakes and rivers in densely forested areas

60 Common Raven · *Corvus corax*

The common raven soars with a wingspan comparable to that of hawk's, travelling along coastlines and over deserts, mountain ridges and arctic tundra. Few birds occupy such a large natural range. • Courting pairs of ravens lock talons and tumble through the air together. These intelligent members of the corvid family maintain loyal, lifelong pair bonds. • Sometimes you will see ravens working as a pair to confiscate a meal. One raven acts as the decoy while the other steals the food.

ID: 1. black upperparts **2.** heavy, black bill **3.** shaggy throat **4.** all-black plumage **5.** wedge-shaped tail
Size: *Length:* 24 in (61 cm); *Wingspan:* 4 ¼ ft (1.3 m)
Where found: coniferous and mixed forests and woodlands; townsites, campgrounds and landfills

Black-capped Chickadee · *Poecile atricapillus*

You can catch a glimpse of the incredibly sociable black-capped chickadee at any time of the year across much of Canada.

In winter, black-caps mix with kinglets, nuthatches, creepers and small woodpeckers; in spring and fall, they join mixed flocks of vireos and warblers. At feeders, you may even be able to entice one to the palm of your hand with the help of a sunflower seed.

• On cold nights, chickadees enter into a hypothermic state, lowering their body temperatures and heartbeats considerably to conserve energy.

ID: 1. black cap **2.** white "cheek" **3.** grey back and wings **4.** white edging on wing feathers **5.** white underparts
Size: *Length:* 5–6 in (13–15 cm); *Wingspan:* 8 in (20 cm)
Where found: deciduous and mixed forests, riparian woodlands, wooded urban parks and backyard feeders

62 Horned Lark · *Eremophila alpestris*

The horned lark's impressive, high-speed, plummeting courtship dive would blow anybody's hair back, or in this bird's case, its two unique black horns. Long before the snow is gone, the lark's tinkling song is one of the first introductions to spring.
• Horned larks are often abundant at roadsides, searching for seeds, but an approaching vehicle usually sends them flying into an adjacent field, making it difficult to identify them. Watch for the blackish tail that contrasts with the sandy-coloured body.

ID: 1. small black "horns" (rarely raised) **2.** light yellow to white face **3.** black line under eye extends from bill to "cheek" **4.** dark tail with white outer tail feathers **5.** black breast band
Size: *Length:* 7 in (18 cm); *Wingspan:* 12 in (30 cm)
Where found: *Breeding:* open areas, including pastures, croplands, airfields and alpine tundra. *In migration and winter:* croplands, roadside ditches and fields

Purple Martin · *Progne subis*

If you set up "condo complexes" for these large swallows, they will entertain you all spring and summer. Martin adults spiral around their nesting sites in pursuit of flying insects, while their young perch clumsily at the cavity openings. Purple martins once nested in natural tree hollows and in cliff crevices but now favour human-made housing. • Martin condos must be cleaned out and closed in autumn to deter the invasion of house sparrows or European starlings.

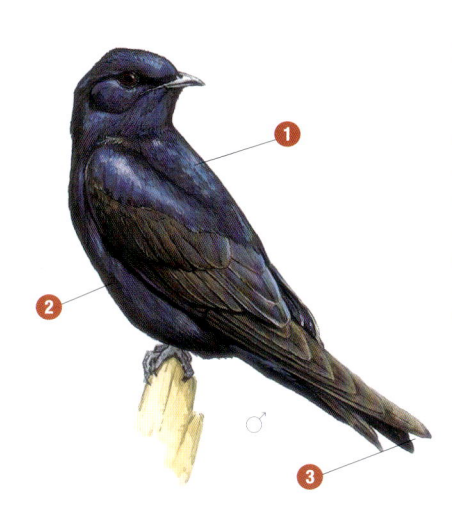

ID: *(male)* **1.** glossy, dark blue body **2.** dark underparts on male **3.** slightly forked tail
Size: *Length:* 7–7 ¾ in (18–20 cm); *Wingspan:* 17 ¾ in (45 cm)
Where found: semi-open areas, often near water

female

64 Barn Swallow · *Hirundo rustica*

Barn swallows once nested on cliffs, but they are now found more frequently nesting on human-made structures. Barns, boathouses and areas under bridges and house eaves all provide shelter from predators and inclement weather. These swallows roll mud into small balls and build their nests one mouthful of mud at a time.
• This swallow is a natural pest controller, feeding on insects that are often harmful to crops and livestock.

ID: 1. rufous throat and forehead **2.** rust- to buff-coloured underparts **3.** long, deeply forked tail
Size: *Length:* 7 in (18 cm); *Wingspan:* 12–13 in (30–33 cm)
Where found: open rural and urban areas where bridges, culverts and buildings are near water

Ruby-crowned Kinglet · *Corthylio calendula*

When engaged in spring courtship or chasing off a rival, the male ruby-crowned kinglet holds its small, ruby crown erect. Throughout most of the year, though, the crown is hidden among the feather-tips atop the bird's head. • During migration, these tiny birds can be seen flitting about treetops, intermingling with warblers and vireos. • The female ruby-crown lays up to 12 eggs, the largest clutch of any North American songbird its size.

ID: 1. short, dark tail **2.** 2 white wing bars **3.** bold, broken eye ring
Male: **4.** male's small, red crown is usually hidden
Size: *Length:* 4 in (10 cm); *Wingspan:* 7 ½ in (19 cm)
Where found: mixed woodlands and pure coniferous forests, especially with spruce; often near wet forest openings and edges

66 Cedar Waxwing · *Bombycilla cedrorum*

The cedar waxwing's yellow tail band and "waxy" red wing tips get their colour from pigments in the berries that this bird eats.
• This waxwing breeds across Canada and has an amusing courtship dance. To attract a mate, the male hops toward a female and offers her a berry. The female accepts the berry and hops away, then returns the berry to the male. • The similar Bohemian waxwing nests farther north and is a year-round resident.

ID: 1. cinnamon crest **2.** black "mask" **3.** small red "drops" on wings **4.** yellow wash on belly **5.** white undertail coverts
Size: *Length:* 7 in (18 cm); *Wingspan:* 12 in (30 cm)
Where found: wooded residential parks and gardens, overgrown fields, forest edges, second-growth, riparian and open woodlands

Red-breasted Nuthatch · *Sitta canadensis* 67

The agile red-breasted nuthatch may look a little like a woodpecker, but it moves down tree trunks headfirst, cleaning up the seeds, insects and nuts that woodpeckers may have overlooked. • The name "nuthatch" comes from this bird's habit of wedging large nuts into crevices, then using its bill to hammer the nuts open.

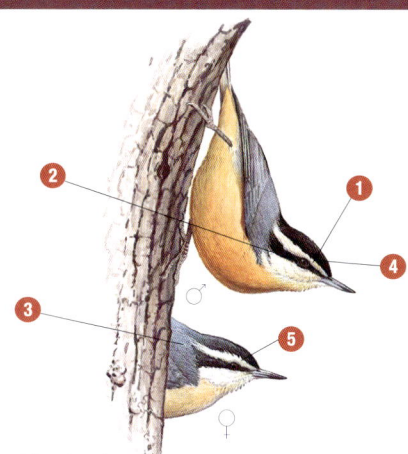

ID: 1. white "eyebrow" 2. black eye line
3. grey blue upperparts
Male: **4.** black crown
Female: **5.** dark grey crown
Size: *Length:* 4 ¼ in (11 cm);
Wingspan: 8 ¼ in (21 cm)
Where found: *Breeding:* spruce–fir and pine forests; pine plantations. *In migration and winter:* mixed woodlands, especially those near bird feeders

68 White-breasted Nuthatch · *Sitta carolinensis*

A number of species—creepers, woodpeckers and nuthatches—are specialized tree gleaners, working tree trunks and limbs in search of bark-dwelling insects. White-breasted nuthatches typically move head first down trunks rather than upwards. This perspective allows them to see into nooks and spot prey that other birds would miss. • Nuthatches are common feeder visitors. Listen for their loud, nasal *yank yank yank* call.

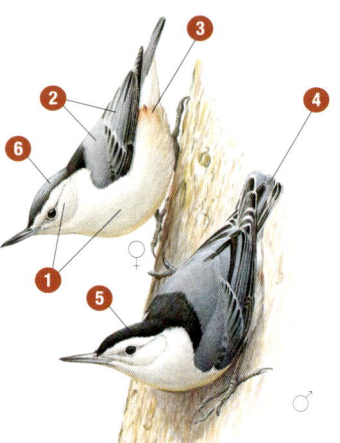

ID: 1. bright white face and breast **2.** blue-grey back and wings **3.** rusty undertail coverts **4.** short tail
Male: **5.** black cap
6. *Female:* greyish cap
Size: *Length:* 4 in (10 cm); *Wingspan:* 8 in (20 cm)
Where found: deciduous and mixed forests, treed residential areas, bird feeders

Brown Creeper · *Certhia americana* 69

The cryptic brown creeper often goes unnoticed until a flake of bark suddenly takes the shape of a bird. A frightened creeper will freeze and flatten itself against a tree trunk, becoming nearly invisible.
• This bird feeds by slowly spiralling up a tree trunk, using its long, stiff tail feathers to prop itself up. When it reaches the upper branches, it floats down to the base of a neighbouring tree to begin another foraging ascent.

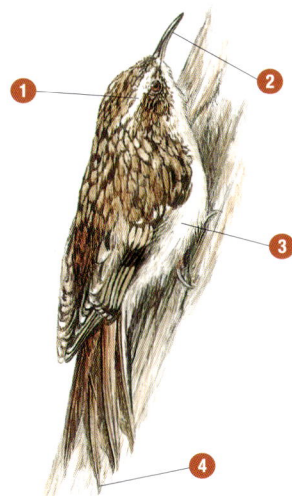

ID: 1. white "eyebrow" **2.** downcurved bill **3.** white underparts **4.** long, pointed tail feathers
Size: *Length:* 5 in (13 cm); *Wingspan:* 7 ½ in (19 cm)
Where found: mature deciduous, coniferous and mixed forests, especially with dead trees

70 House Wren · *Troglodytes aedon*

The house wren usually carries its short, finely barred tail tilted upward. • You might overlook this tiny bird until you hear it's sweet, melodious song. • Despite its bubbly warble, this wren can be very aggressive toward other species that nest in its territory. It might even puncture and toss eggs from other birds' nests. • House wrens often build numerous nests, which later serve as decoys or "dummy" nests to fool would-be enemies.

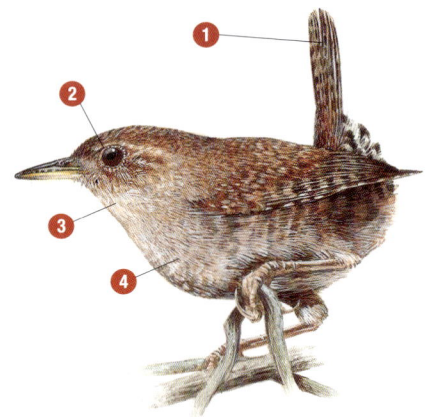

ID: 1. short, upraised tail finely barred with black **2.** faint, pale "eyebrow" and eye ring **3.** whitish throat **4.** whitish to buff underparts
Size: *Length:* 4 ¾ in (12 cm); *Wingspan:* 5 ½ in (14 cm)
Where found: thickets and shrubby openings in or at the edge of deciduous or mixed woodlands; often in shrubs and thickets near buildings

Gray Catbird · *Dumetella carolinensis*

The gray catbird is an accomplished mimic. You may hear it shuffling through underbrush and dense riparian shrubs, calling its catlike meow. The gray catbird's ability to use both sides of its syrinx allows it to sing two notes at once. • This bird vigilantly defends its territory and will destroy the eggs and nestlings of other songbirds. The female can recognize the egg of a brown-headed cowbird and will remove it from her nest.

ID: 1. black cap **2.** long tail is dark grey to black **3.** chestnut undertail coverts **4.** dark plumage overall
Size: *Length:* 8 ¾ in (22 cm); *Wingspan:* 11 in (28 cm)
Where found: dense thickets, brambles, shrubby or brushy areas and hedgerows, often near water

72 European Starling · *Sturnus vulgaris*

The European starling spread across North America after being released in New York's Central Park in the 1890s. This highly adaptable bird not only took over the nesting sites of native cavity nesters but also learned to mimic the calls of other birds. • Look for massive evening roosts of European starlings under bridges or on buildings. • These birds have a variable diet that includes destructive agricultural pests, berries, grains and even human food waste.

breeding

nonbreeding

ID: 1. iridescent, purple black head and neck 2. glossy, green back with buffy spots 3. greenish black underparts 4. yellow bill
Size: *Length:* 8 ¾ in (22 cm); *Wingspan:* 16 ¼ in (41 cm)
Where found: agricultural areas, townsites, woodland edges, landfills and roadsides

Eastern Bluebird · need name

Look for this small, brightly coloured thrush perched on fence posts or overhead wires near open fields. • Bluebirds are cavity nesters and face fierce competition for natural nest cavities from more aggressive species, including the introduced European starling and house sparrow. Fortunately, bluebird enthusiasts have developed "bluebird trails," nest boxes mounted on fence posts and utility poles stretching along highways and rural roads. These boxes are too small for the starling to access and provide the bluebird with convenient nesting places, which has greatly bolstered their populations.

ID: *Male:* **1.** rusty red throat, breast and sides **2.** white belly and undertail coverts **3.** dark bill **4.** deep blue upperparts
Size: *Length:* 7 in (18 cm); *Wingspan:* 13 in (33 cm)
Where found: open country with scattered trees and fence lines; forest clearings and edges; golf courses and cemeteries; often near bluebird nest boxes

American Robin · *Turdus migratorius*

Come spring, the familiar song of the American robin may wake you early if you are a light sleeper. This abundant bird adapts easily to urban areas and often works from dawn until after dusk when there is a nest to be built or hungry, young mouths to feed. • The robin's bright red belly contrasted with its dark head and wings make this bird easy to identify even for a nonbirder. • Warmer weather, open water springs and fermenting fruit convince more and more robins to stay the winter each year.

ID: 1. black head **2.** incomplete white eye ring **3.** white undertail coverts
Male: **4.** deep brick red breast
Female: **5.** light red-orange breast
Size: *Length:* 10 in (25 cm); *Wingspan:* 17 in (43 cm)
Where found: residential lawns and gardens, pastures, urban parks, broken forests, bogs and river shorelines

House Sparrow · *Passer domesticus* 75

breeding

A black "mask" and "bib" adorn the male of this adaptive, aggressive species. The house sparrow's tendency to usurp territory has led to a decline in native bird populations. This sparrow helps itself to other bird's homes, such as a bluebird or cliff swallow nest or a purple martin house. • This abundant, conspicuous bird was introduced to North America in the 1850s as part of a plan to control the insects that were damaging grain and cereal crops. As it turns out, these birds are largely vegetarian!

nonbreeding

ID: *Male:* **1.** black lores and "bib" **2.** chestnut nape extends to eye **3.** light grey "cheek" *Female:* **4.** buffy "eyebrow"
Size: *Length:* 5 ½–6 in (14–15 cm); *Wingspan:* 9 ½ in (24 cm)
Where found: townsites, urban and suburban areas, farmyards and agricultural areas, railway yards and other developed areas

76 Evening Grosbeak · *Coccothraustes vespertinus*

Anyone with a winter bird feeder knows the appetite of evening grosbeaks; a small flock can devour a tray of sunflower seeds in no time. Scattering husks and unopen seeds, the birds often create an unplanned sunflower garden that is discovered the following spring. • Large eruptions of evening grosbeaks occur every two or three years but in many parts of the country winter populations are diminishing. Breeding bird surveys also show declines in Canada of more than 5 percent per year since 1980.

ID: 1. large, conical, yellowish bill
2. conspicuous white wing patch
3. dark wings **4.** short tail
Male: **5.** dark olive-brown head and throat
Female: **6.** greyish brown upper back and head
Size: *Length:* 7–8 in (18–20 cm); *Wingspan:* 13 in (33 cm)
Where found: *Breeding:* mixed coniferous forests. *In migration and winter:* open hardwood forests

Purple Finch · *Haemorhous purpureus*

Despite its name, the purple finch's plumage is more raspberry red rather than purple. • Its musical *pik* call is given frequently and is a good way to know if this finch is nearby. • A flat, raised, table-style feeding station and nearby tree cover are sure to attract purple finches, and a feeder may keep a small flock in your area over winter. • In breeding season, the male dances around the female, beating his wings rapidly until he gracefully lifts into the air.

ID: *Male:* **1.** raspberry red wash over most of body **2.** pale, unstreaked underparts **3.** pale, conical bill
Female: **4.** white "eyebrow" and lower "cheek" stripe **5.** heavily streaked underparts
Size: *Length:* 5–6 in (13–15 cm); *Wingspan:* 10 in (25 cm)
Where found: *Breeding:* coniferous and mixed forests. *In migration and winter:* coniferous, mixed and deciduous forests, shrubby open areas and feeders

78 Common Redpoll · *Acanthis flammea*

Common redpoll numbers vary each winter. Sometimes small groups show up, and other years, they might appear in flocks of hundreds. Watch for redpolls gleaning waste grain from bare fields or stocking up at winter feeders. • Common redpolls are at risk of freezing in cold temperatures. These birds stay warm by fluffing their feathers, creating an insulating layer of warm air.

nonbreeding

ID: 1. red forecrown 2. black "chin" 3. notched tail
Female: 4. whitish to pale grey breast
Male: 5. pinkish red breast
Size: *Length:* 5 in (13 cm); *Wingspan:* 9 in (23 cm)
Where found: open fields and meadows; along roadsides, utility power lines, railways, forest edges; backyards with feeders

Pine Siskin · *Spinus pinus*

Pine siskins fluctuate in abundance both seasonally and with availability of their favourite food sources. They are usually most common in fall, winter and spring. Siskins eat niger seeds in great quantities and can rapidly deplete your feeder. It is important to maintain dry seed—rain-soaked seed can rot, causing salmonella outbreaks which may incapacitate or kill feeder-dependent birds.

ID: 1. indistinct facial pattern **2.** dull whitish wing bars **3.** yellow at base of tail and in wings **4.** heavily streaked underparts **5.** slightly forked tail
Size: *Length:* 4–5 in (10–13 cm); *Wingspan:* 8–9 in (20–23 cm)
Where found: *Breeding:* coniferous and hardwood forests; exotic plantations. *In migration and winter:* any natural or human-influenced habitat

80 American Goldfinch · *Spinus tristis*

It is hard to miss the American goldfinches' jubilant call and distinctive, undulating flight style as they flutter over weedy fields and gardens and along roadsides. • Because these acrobatic birds regularly feed while hanging upside down, finch feeders have been designed with the seed opening below the perch. These feeders discourage more aggressive house sparrows from stealing the seeds. Use niger or millet seeds to attract American goldfinches to your bird feeder.

breeding

ID: 1. black wings and tail
Male: **2.** black cap extends onto forehead
Female: **3.** yellow-green upperparts
 Size: *Length:* 5 ½ in (14 cm);
Wingspan: 9 ½ in (24 cm)
Where found: weedy fields, woodland edges

Dark-eyed Junco · *Junco hyemalis*

You may spot dark-eyed juncos scratching at the leaves under your feeder. These birds prefer to feed on the ground, avoiding the crowd of chickadees, nuthatches and jays. • The dark-eyed junco has 15 easily recognizable subspecies. In Canada, these subspecies are grouped into either the mostly grey "slate-coloured" junco or the brown-sided, black-headed "Oregon" junco. • These sparrows breed in the north and are found year-round in central and south-western Canada. In severe weather, they fold their feet under their bodies and fluff out their feathers on the snow like a quilt.

"Slate-coloured"

ID: "Slate-coloured" junco **1.** pale, conical bill **2.** white outer tail feathers **3.** dark slate grey overall **4.** white breast, belly and undertail coverts
Size: *Length:* 6 in (15 cm); *Wingspan:* 9 ½ in (24 cm)
Where found: *Breeding:* coniferous and mixed forests; shrubby, regenerating areas. *In migration and winter:* shrubby woodland borders, backyard feeders

"Oregon"

82 Chipping Sparrow · *Chipping sparrow*

The chipping sparrow can be easily distinguished from other sparrows by its bright rufous cap. • This sparrow builds its nest at eye level or lower in a tree or shrub. It prefers conifers as a nesting site and uses hair as lining material. The nest is often so poorly constructed and flimsy that the eggs can be seen through the nest materials. • A small percentage of male chipping sparrows are polygynous, meaning that one male may have two females sitting on separate clutches at the same time.

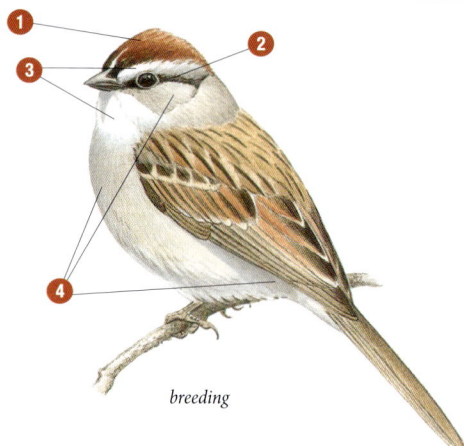

breeding

ID: *Breeding:* **1.** rufous cap **2.** black eyeline **3.** white eyebrow and throat **4.** grey nape, rump and underparts
Size: *Length:* 5 ½ in (14 cm); *Wingspan:* 8 ¼ in (21 cm)
Where found: open conifers or mixed-wood land edges with young trees or shrubs to subalpine forests; often in yards and gardens with tree and shrub borders

White-throated Sparrow · *Zonotrichia albicollis*

Even if you haven't seen the white-throated sparrow, you have likely heard its simple *dear sweet Canada Canada Canada* song. • Two colour phases are common throughout Canada: one has black and white stripes on its head, whereas the other has brown and tan stripes. White-striped males are more aggressive than tan-striped males, and tan-striped females are more nurturing than are white-striped birds. • Look for this sparrow scratching patches of leaf litter in search of food.

"white-striped"

"tan-striped"

ID: 1. white throat **2.** black eye line **3.** black crown with bold white median stripe and eyebrow **4.** bright yellow lores
Size: *Length:* 6–7 in (15–18 cm); *Wingspan:* 9 in (23 cm)
Where found: *Breeding:* shrubby, semi-open forests, regenerating clearings and shrubby forest edges. *In migration and winter:* shrubby edge habitats and suburban yards

84 Song Sparrow · *Melospiza melodia*

Although its plumage is unremarkable, the appropriately named song sparrow is among the great singers of the bird world. By the time a young male is a few months old, he has created a courtship tune of his own, having learned the basics of melody and rhythm from his father and male rivals. Female songbirds are not usually vocal, but the female song sparrow will occasionally sing a tune of her own. • In breeding season, pairs of song sparrows raise as many as three or four families.

ID: 1. dark crown with pale central stripe
2. dark "moustache" stripes **3.** white jaw line
4. heavy brown streaks converge at central breast spot
Size: *Length:* 5 ½ in (14 cm);
Wingspan: 8 in (20 cm)
Where found: willow shrublands, riparian thickets, forest openings and pastures, all often near water

Eastern Meadowlark · *Sturnella magna* 85

Most female birds have drab plumage to camouflage them during the breeding season, but the female eastern meadowlark uses a different strategy. She shares the V-shaped necklace and bright yellow throat and belly of her male counterpart, but for a slightly different purpose—an incubating female will burst from the grass, creating a colourful distraction to lead predators away from the nest. • Listen for this bird's proud song whistled from the fence posts and powerlines in rural areas.

ID: **1.** mottled brown upperparts **2.** long, sharp bill **3.** broad, black breast band **4.** short, wide tail with white outer tail feathers **5.** long, pinkish legs **6.** yellow underparts
Size: *Length:* 9–9 ½ in (23–24 cm); *Wingspan:* 14 in (36 cm)
Where found: grassy meadows and pastures, croplands, weedy fields, grassy roadsides and old orchards

86 Baltimore Oriole · *Icterus galbula*

With a robin-like song and a preference for the canopies of neighbourhood trees, the Baltimore oriole is difficult to spot. A hanging pouch nest dangling in a bare tree in fall is sometimes the only evidence the bird was there at all. • Orioles breed in the Prairies and across southeastern Canada, then fly south for winter. Their nests are very strong and often remain intact through the harshest winters. • At first glance, this oriole can be confused with the Bullock's oriole, which is found in southern BC, Alberta and southwestern Saskatchewan.

ID: *Male:* **1.** 2 white wing bands **2.** bright orange underparts.
Female: **3.** white wing band and feather edgings **4.** dull yellow orange underparts and rump
Size: *Length:* 7–8 in (18–20 cm); *Wingspan:* 11 in (28 cm)
Where found: deciduous and mixed forests, particularly riparian woodlands, natural openings, shorelines, roadsides, orchards, gardens and parklands

Red-winged Blackbird · *Agelaius phoeniceus*

The male red-winged blackbird wears his bright red shoulders like armour—together with his short, raspy song, they are key to defending his territory from rivals. In field experiments, males whose red shoulders were painted black soon lost their territories. • It isn't hard to spot the polygynous males perched on cattails in roadside ditches and wetlands, but the cryptically coloured females usually remain hidden on their nests.

ID: *Male:* **1.** red shoulder patch edged in yellow **2.** black overall
Female: **3.** mottled brown upperparts **4.** heavily streaked underparts **5.** pale "eyebrow."
Size: *Length:* 7–9 in (18–23 cm);
Wingspan: 12–13 in (30–33 cm)
Where found: cattail marshes, wet meadows and ditches, croplands and shoreline shrub

88 Brown-headed Cowbird · *Molothrus ater*

The nomadic brown-headed cowbirds historically followed bison herds across the prairies. The birds do not build their own nests, but instead lay their eggs in other birds' nests. Unsuspecting mothers are left to incubate the cowbird eggs and raise the aggressive young. Orioles, warblers, vireos and tanagers are among the most affected. • Increased livestock farming and fragmentation of forests have encouraged the expansion of the cowbird's range, and it now parasitizes more than 140 bird species.

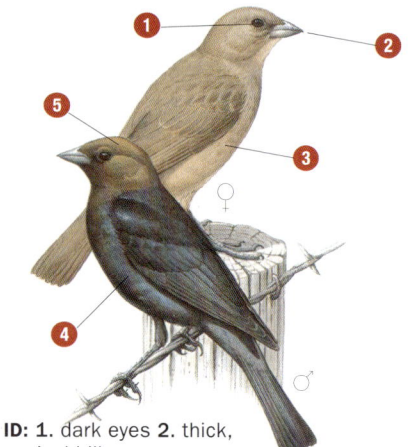

ID: 1. dark eyes **2.** thick, conical bill
Female: **3.** light brown underparts with faint streaking
Male: **4.** iridescent, green blue body plumage appears glossy black **5.** dark brown head
Size: *Length:* 6–8 in (15–20 cm); *Wingspan:* 12 in (30 cm)
Where found: fields, woodland edges, transmission corridors, landfills, parks and areas near cattle

Common Grackle · *Quiscalus quiscula*

Our largest blackbirds, common grackles are abundant and are seen in numbers on every outing. Males are striking birds with a colourful iridescence that gleams in the sun. • Farmers detest grackles because the birds pull up new shoots. • Grackles often form enormous roosts in fall and winter with other blackbirds and European starlings; some roosts number into the hundreds of thousands of birds.

ID: 1. yellow eyes **2.** long, sturdy, dark bill **3.** long, keeled tail
Male: **4.** iridescent plumage, bronze back and sides **5.** purplish head, wings and tail.
Female: **6.** less iridescent plumage
Size: *Length:* 9–9 ½ in (23–24 cm); *Wingspan:* 14 in (36 cm)
Where found: nearly all habitats, especially in open to semi open areas

Common Yellowthroat · *Geothlypis trichas*

This wood-warbler prefers marshlands and wet, overgrown meadows instead of forests. In spring and early summer, look for males perched atop tall cattails or shrubs, singing their *witchety witchety* song. • Common yellowthroats migrate to western Canada in May and leave in September to return to their southern wintering grounds.
• Despite its bright colours and abundance in wetlands, this bird can be difficult to find. Look for them gleaning vegetation for insects and other invertebrates.

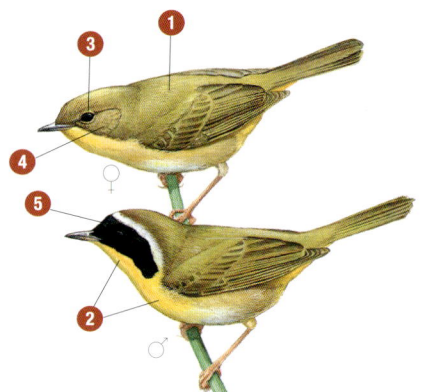

ID: 1. olive green to olive brown upperparts.
2. bright yellow throat and breast
Female: **3.** may show faint, white eye ring
4. no "mask"
Male: **5.** broad, black "mask" with white upper border
Size: *Length:* 5 in (13 cm);
Wingspan: 6 ¼ in (16 cm)
Where found: cattail and bulrush marshes, sedge wetlands, riparian areas, beaver ponds and wet, overgrown meadows; sometimes forages in dry fields

American Redstart · *Setophaga ruticilla* 91

Hyperactive American redstarts constantly flick their wings and fan their tails. It is thought that by flashing the bright orange or yellow spots in their plumage, they flush insects from foliage. • A broad bill and rictal bristles (the short, whisker-like feathers around its mouth) help this bird capture insects in the manner of a flicker. • The orange marks are replaced with yellow on females and first year males, so if you see a "yellowstart" singing, it is a young male.

ID: *Female:* **1.** yellow foreshoulder, wing and tail patches; *Male:* **2.** black head and upperparts **3.** reddish orange foreshoulder, wing and tail patches
Size: *Length:* 5 in (13 cm); *Wingspan:* 7 in (18 cm)
Where found: dense shrubby understorey of deciduous woodlands, often near water

92 Yellow Warbler · *Setophaga petechia*

The yellow warbler is often parasitized by the brown-headed cowbird and can recognize cowbird eggs. Rather than tossing them out, it will build another nest overtop the old eggs or abandon the first nest completely. Occasionally, cowbirds strike repeatedly—a stack of five warbler nests was once found! • The yellow warbler is often mistakenly thought to be a "wild canary." It flits from branch to branch in search of juicy caterpillars, aphids and beetles.

breeding

ID: 1. black bill and eyes **2.** bright yellow body
Male: **3.** red breast streaks
Female: **4.** faint, red breast streaks
Size: *Length:* 5 in (13 cm);
Wingspan: 7 ½ in (19 cm)
Where found: moist, open woodlands with dense, low scrub; shrubby areas, fencerows and riparian woodlands; usually near water

Scarlet Tanager · *Piranga olivacea*

The male scarlet tanager glows neon red, it's scarlet body contrasting with shiny black wings and tail. • Tanagers spend most of their time high in the forest canopy. Knowing their song helps in locating them. Their tune is a raspy whistled series of phrases sounding like an American robin with a sore throat. Most winter in the jungles of South America.

breeding

ID: *Breeding male:* **1.** bright red body
2. pale bill
Female: **3.** pure black wings and tail
4. olive upperparts
Size: *Length:* 7 in (18 cm);
Wingspan: 12 in (30 cm)
Where found: fairly mature, upland deciduous and mixed forests

94 Northern Cardinal · *Cardinalis cardinalis*

An excited or agitated male northern cardinal will display his unforgettable, vibrant red head crest and raise his tail. This colourful year-round resident will vigorously defend his territory, even attacking his own reflection in a window! • Cardinals maintain strong pair bonds. Some couples sing to each other year-round, while others join loose flocks, re-establishing pair bonds in the spring during a "courtship feeding." A male offers a seed to the female, which she then accepts and eats.

ID: 1. red, conical bill
Male: **2.** pointed crest **3.** red overall
4. black "mask" and throat;
Female: **5.** brownish buff overall
Size: *Length:* 7 ½–9 in (19–23 cm); *Wingspan:* 12 in (30 cm)
Where found: brushy thickets and shrubby tangles along forest and woodland edges; backyards and urban and suburban parks

Indigo Bunting · *Passerina cyanea* 95

The vivid, electric blue male indigo bunting is one of the most spectacularly coloured birds in eastern Canada. • These buntings arrive in May, choosing raspberry thickets as favoured nesting sites. Dense, thorny stems keep most predators away and the berries are a good food source. • The male is a persistent singer, vocalizing even throughout the heat of a summer day. Young males learn their couplet songs from neighbouring males during their first year on their own.

breeding

ID: 1. grey, conical bill
Breeding male: **2.** bright blue overall
Female: **3.** soft brown overall
Size: *Length:* 5 ½ in (14 cm); *Wingspan:* 8 in (20 cm)
Where found: deciduous forest and woodland edges, regenerating forest clearings, orchards and shrubby fields

© 2023 by Partners Publishing Ltd.

All rights reserved. No part of this work covered by the copyrights hereon may be reproduced or used in any form or by any means—graphic, electronic or mechanical—or stored in a retrieval system or transmitted in any form by any means without the prior written permission of the publisher, except for reviewers, who may quote brief passages. Any request for photocopying, recording, taping or storage on information retrieval systems of any part of this work shall be directed in writing to the publisher.

Distributed by: **Canada Book Distributors - Booklogic**
www.canadabookdistributors.com
Tel: 1-800-661-9017

Canadian Cataloguing in Publication Data

Title: Eastern Canada birds / contributors: Krista Kagume, Gregory Kennedy, Roger Burrows, Andy Bezener. Other titles: Eastern birds Names: Kagume, Krista, contributor. | Kennedy, Gregory, 1956- contributor. | Burrows, Roger, 1942- contributor. | Bezener, Andy, 1971- contributor.

Description: Also published under the title: Eastern birds. Identifiers: Canadiana 20240317505 | ISBN 9781772131291 (softcover) Subjects: LCSH: Birds—Canada, Eastern—Identification. | LCSH: Birds—East (U.S.)—Identification. | LCSH: Bird watching—Canada, Eastern. | LCSH: Bird watching—East (U.S.) | LCGFT: Field guides. Classification: LCC QL681 .E28 2024b | DDC 598.097—dc23

Title: Eastern birds / contributors: Krista Kagume, Gregory Kennedy, Roger Burrows, Andy Bezener. Names: Kagume, Krista, contributor. | Kennedy, Gregory, 1956- contributor. | Burrows, Roger, 1942- contributor. | Bezener, Andy, 1971- contributor.

Description: Also published under the title: Eastern Canada birds. Identifiers: Canadiana 20240317491 | ISBN 9781772131338 (softcover) Subjects: LCSH: Birds—Canada, Eastern—Identification. | LCSH: Birds—East (U.S.)—Identification. | LCSH: Bird watching—Canada, Eastern. | LCSH: Bird watching—East (U.S.) | LCGFT: Field guides. Classification: LCC QL681 .E28 2024 | DDC 598.097—dc23

Contributors: Krista Kagume, Gregory Kennedy, Roger Burrows, Andy Bezener

We acknowledge the financial support of the Government of Canada.
Nous reconnaissons l'appui financier du gouvernement du Canada.

Funded by the Government of Canada
Financé par le gouvernement du Canada | **Canadä**

Printed in China
PC: 38-1